The Single Christian

Tiffany Simone

Maximize Publishing Inc.

2018 Monterey Ave

Bronx N.Y. 10457

Attn.: Michael McCain

C/o: Kevin Brown

Kelby Lott

For Author: Tiffany Simone

ISBN-13:
978-0692264317 (Maximize Publishing Inc.)

ISBN-10:
0692264310 Retail Price: 15.99

Table of Contents:

Dedication..9

Preface..11

Introduction..13

The Single Christian..21

About The Author..103

The Single Christian

Tiffany Simone

Dedication

To every person who said yes to God

It was so beautiful but one day got really hard

Everyone found love except for you

You've prayed and cried, what's left to do?

Wait...but for how long?

I'm weak and pretend to be strong

I don't know how much longer I can hold on

God you used to hear me but it seems like you've gone

For those of you who've prayed countless prayers

For those of you who've cried countless tears

For those of you who feel God doesn't care

For those of you who think Gods no longer there

For those of you who spend your weekends at home

For those of you who spend your free time alone

God wants your joy to be true

Single Christian this one is for you.

Preface

Dr. Michael McCain

The Single Christian by Tiffany Simone is one of the most powerful books on Christian Life Style and living I have had yet to read. When I think of all the joys and trials of love and relationships allot of the topics covered in this book bring thought provoking concepts and insights. The author offers Godly tips and advice both in dating and relationships. Tiffany Simone is a voice the body of Christ and adults of all ages have been longing for.

When you get this book in hand, get ready to have your mind and spirit renewed! Get ready for the author's candid transparency and a look into the life of a young woman both sharing her wisdom and insight on how to live the "Saved single Christian life".

Enjoy!

Introduction

"Don't worry; God is going to heal you. He will take care of every hurt that you've ever experienced. He is the Balm in Gilead, He is the Alpha and Omega and God is using the things that you have been through to make you stronger, wiser and bring you closer to Him. He will heal every hurt and wash every tear away", is what I said to her. I believed that with all of my heart, God mends the broken hearted and fills every void in our life and is able to complete us and heal us in a way that is impossible for man to do.

However, she quickly rebuked me. "No! I don't receive that. I don't want *God* to heal me; I want God to send a man to heal me. See, people don't believe that God will use a person to minister to that hurt but He will. God is going to send a man that will love me, take care of me and my child and treat me the way I am supposed to be treated. God is going to send a man to heal me, I deserve it after all the hell that I've been through". This is before her divorce papers were filed.

In the eyes of God and the United States she was still a married woman. Her marriage had been tumultuous and instead of seeking God for healing, she believed God began to show her next husband before she was even divorced. The one who would heal her and make every tear she had to cry in distress worth it. Am I the only one that sees something wrong with this picture? What would have been so wrong with getting a divorce and being a single Christian...getting closer with God and using what you've been through to gain personal wisdom and impart into others? Why are Christians so against being single? I've counseled women of all ages, some even in their 60's and they all have this "I'm waiting on my husband" syndrome. So it's not just partial to Christians in a certain age group, it can literally be anyone, even your grandmother, that still has issues with being a single Christian.

The thing about putting all of your hope and trust into a human is that, we change. It's like deciding to build your house on sand. Sure its stable and gets the job done for now, but if the wind blows too hard or the rain begins to fall your foundation or the very thing you based your healing in is gone. People change, we are in a very temporary state on earth and we go through many phases while in this earthen state that prepare us for our eternal state. Sure I'm with you today, but tomorrow your issues will be too much for me to bear. Of course I'll try to understand you today, but tomorrow you'll begin to sound crazy. Face it that is how some of us can be. That is why it can be dangerous to our spirit, mind and emotions to expect healing from another human. When we begin to desire a person rather than God, something is terribly wrong. God is immutable, He never changes and He is the only One strong enough and Loving enough to stay by our side everyday of our life no matter what happens and not change His opinion about us or give up on us.

To be honest, the counseling that I've done, the countless stories of long lost loves that I've heard about the one who got away, the one God wanted me to marry but haters blocked it, the one who was supposed to be with me but wouldn't get saved etc., turned me off! I was sick of hearing about people who knew the Love of God and had His Spirit at their fingertips act as if God wasn't enough. We of all people should find happiness in God alone, He's what makes us different from the world and He should be our all and all no matter who is or isn't in our lives. So I said, "God, I don't want to get married. I just want you. I'll show all of these relationship obsessed people!

They think your relationship status defines you. Well, I'll be single in the natural, happy, at peace, preoccupied, Spiritual and proud!" It takes a carnal mind to think that our relationship status being single really makes us single. If God said that He'd never leave us and that He'd be with us always even unto the end of the world....are we truly single? I'd rather be single in the natural and coupled up with the Holy Ghost in the spirit any day! Sadly, a lot of us would rather be coupled up in the natural and single in the spirit. I love my Father, He saved my life....how dare people look past this Super Being, the One Who died for us, the One Who dwells with us, the One who loves us, because He's not "enough". Well, if God can't satisfy us, then no one can! What causes this un-satisfaction with God while we're single? Maybe its embarrassment, maybe its low self-esteem, maybe it's our carnality, maybe it's our maturity level or maybe it's all of the above.

As single Christians most of us have the Genesis 2:18-25 syndrome...we don't like to be alone and expect to close our eyes, say a prayer and open them to our perfect match, soul mate or other half to have instantly appeared. There is so much help for married Christians: counseling, retreats, marriage groups, countless scriptures etc. It can feel like us single Christians are told not to fornicate and we are on our own from there. We struggle with whom to date, when to date and how to date, we also struggle with this thought "what if I never get married".

When I decided to live for God, for various different reasons I decided not to put any thought or effort into dating and to submit all of my faculties unto the Lord. I thought if God had someone for me then I would meet them at the right time. We watch people in our lives become engaged and get married and it seems like that type of love is for everyone else but you. Hey God...did you forget about me before the foundation of the earth when you were pairing people together? What if God just wanted you paired with Him in life, would that be so bad? I've counseled people who wanted love more than God. God wants your heart; you have to seek Him first before He begins to add potential distractions to your life. This book does 7 things:

1: The Single Christian shows you how to read between the lines in the scriptures and extract everything that will help you as you serve God. Guess what scriptures currently apply to you.....all of them except for the ones for people who are already married. I even encourage you to study the scriptures on marriage; even though you aren't married and may never be married it is very important for you to know the Word of God in its entirety.

2: The Single Christian encourages you to have a deep, personal and intimate relationship with God before searching for a mate.

3: The Single Christians purpose is to get you on the road to being the best single Christian you can be, whether God has a spouse for you or not.

4: The Single Christian implores you to trust Gods plan for your life, even if you don't understand it.

5: The Single Christian causes you to take a look at your life and raises the question, with your circle of friends, habits, mindset, financial situation etc., Are you truly ready for marriage?

6: The Single Christian gives you tips and advice on what you can do to have a happy successful marriage in the future.

7: The Single Christian encourages you to love God completely and follow His Word entirely.

May the seed planted in your life through this book blossom in to something beautiful. Enjoy!!

The Single Christian

I was a church baby! I attended church every Sunday with my grandmother, who was an evangelist and later became a minister and older brother while my mom worked. Even though I went to church every Sunday I had only basic knowledge of God. Nine out of ten churches limit the information, study of doctrine and participation of children to "kid friendly" things. Thus limiting their level of spirituality, this is why there are so many people who can grow up in church and go astray when they get to a certain age. They were never really grounded and rooted in the Word of God; they grew up in church but never grew up in Christ. The seed was planted but they do not submit their selves enough to be watered, and I was becoming one of these people.

To be honest by the time I was 12 or 13 years old I was growing up and also growing tired of "church". There was no doubt that God was real however my lack of intimacy with Him and knowledge of who He really is made it impossible for me to want a real relationship with Him. As I aged into a teenager I began to grow into a free spirit however, I stayed grounded in the basic principles of what was morally right and wrong that I learned growing up in church. I clearly remember being a pre-teen and a teenager and watching the Maury Show and Jerry Springer and praying that I would never be as naive as the women I saw on TV. I would pray "please give me wisdom God", I never wanted to find myself not knowing the obvious signs of cheating or if a man loved me or not or who the father of my child was.

Little did I know that God would answer my prayer, not just by giving me the spiritual gift of discernment but by allowing me to date ALL types of men and make it out of many situations that most women have not made it out of. The wisdom that I prayed for only comes through experience. You don't really know about a particular thing until you have to go through it. Then comes the much desired wisdom and not so desired gray hair. God allowing me to go through these extreme experiences (that I choose not to go into detail about...it would be another book in itself and not a nice one might I add) has enabled me to be wise in this area of life and even now God uses me to give advice to women who are old enough to be my mother and even grandmother concerning their relationships.

But back to me growing up, I was a free spirit; I did what I wanted to do whenever I felt like doing it. I've dated men from all walks of life from pimps (yes real pimps, can't date them for too long....can you say aggressive?) to erudite scholars and every type of sane and not so sane man in between. Some of these guys were even old enough to be my father. The hurt, joy, love and fear that I felt from my romantic occurrences resulted in me maturing and becoming the friend that always had the best advice. I was conscious of the fact that I was experiencing a lot and I made it a point to take away all the wisdom that I could from every failed relationship.

My motto became "it won't happen to me twice", in my opinion there is no point in going through a hardship or life changing experience if you don't learn from it. Furthermore each time you come out of a bad relationship you have to step your game up so you don't become that person who goes through the same things over and over constantly making the same mistakes. My experiences dating enabled me to develop a higher standard for whoever I dated as the years passed.

A family friend had a church fairly close to my home; I love her and her preaching so I decided to go back to church in my early twenties. This time around I developed a real hunger for the Word of God and began to study it and read it day and night. I began to live my life according to the Word, I made the necessary changes and I was faithful in my attendance to church. Soon after I became a deaconess at the church I was a member of and enrolled in Seminary school as a Theology major. Due to an ex-boyfriend, some unfortunate circumstances at the church I went to and me being a baby in the spirit, I backslid.

My faith wasn't strong and I wasn't knowledgeable enough in the Word to be successful and faithful to God through trails. I needed to grow in the Spirit and be led to the church home that God had for me. A couple of years after I backslid I had even more unfortunate experiences in the world which led me back to the Lord....but on my own terms. I didn't have a church home, I would inconsistently drop off my tithes at a friend's church, and I read the Word and dropped some proclivities. Obviously doing things your own way can never work. When you are building your relationship with the Lord you have to hear His Word. Your faith is established and strengthened through hearing the Word of God (Romans 10:17) you also have to live by His Word even if it is outside of your comfort zone. I wanted to stay within my comfort zone and this stubbornness and ignorance denoted me clinging to my flesh.

So of course my new "relationship" with God fell off track again!! So I went head first back into my old lifestyle. Time passed and even though I was not living according to the commandments of God, I surprisingly began to do well. I attended a great church from time to time (but wasn't a member), I had a full time city job working with grade school children and a part time retail job (with a fabulous discount might I add) and I was happy. At that time I also dated really nice, accomplished, chivalrous men.

My past experiences paid off and I cleaved to the standards that I had for who I dated, I did not for one second compromise or depreciate my former happenings for anyone. I remember that it was at this point in my life I began to operate in spiritual gifts like I never had before, discerning of spirits, prophesying to people and having prophetic dreams, sensing and smelling demons and hearing the voice of God like I never had before. It was a little overwhelming for me but it wasn't enough to make me completely give my life to God. It wasn't completely new but what made it worthy of mention is that at this particular point in my life I was not in control of my gifts and it was deeper than anything I had ever experienced.

I always operated in prophecy (when I didn't know any better I considered myself to be psychic), discernment (again I was in a sinful state and discernment was perceived as me being a "Miss Know it All) and I experienced supernatural occurrences would that would scar most normal people. These were all a few of the gifts that I was born with and I didn't understand them or how to operate in them until I grew up in the Spirit. One spring day I received a phone call from a prophet telling me that this was my season, God wanted to use me and to go to my secret closet and pray for everything from my career to my husband.

So that's just what I did. I prayed that God would lead me into a career that would provide a comfortable life for my family, I prayed that whoever my husband would be, he'd be a great support system and able to handle the spiritually gifted person God created me to be. I prayed on my face for many things in great detail. God let me know that this was it, it was my time to give my all to Him and for some reason I didn't fight against God or run from Him. I was ready to live the life that God had for me. I was humbled that He reached out to me and I answered the call that was on my life with a big YES!

So it wasn't long after this phone call that I stopped dating because I wanted God to be my main focus, I felt like God deserved all of my time and emotion. I did not want any distractions; I wanted to get it right this time around. I felt like I had wasted so much of my life with foolishness that I went head first into my destiny with God, trying to redeem myself of all the time that I had wasted. However, I later learned that this time wasn't really wasted, it made for an even greater testimony and geared me for my line of ministry, it also gave me the ability to reach and relate to people that most "church folk" could not.

I attended church regularly and became quite active in ministry; I studied the Word, enrolled back in Seminary school and began my whirlwind love story and destiny with the Lord. One spring morning about a year after I became completely sold out for God, I walked up the steps to my job as an Assistant

Teacher. I remember praying and being very adamant about not wanting to date and not wanting to waste my time with a man who wasn't going to be my husband. My time is irreplaceable and very precious to me and at that point in my life I really didn't want to date anyone furthermore I didn't care whether I got married or not as long as I stayed in the will of God.

I remember praying as I walked up the steps and saying, God I'm not wasting my time and talking to just any 'ole body, the next man I give my number to is going to be my husband. I walked into the classroom, sat at my desk and about 5 minutes later there was a knock at the door. Standing there was a 6'4 brown skin, clean cut young man who was VERY attractive! He was there to fix the teachers laptop that I worked with and him and I being left alone in the classroom began to talk. I asked him if he went to church, he said yes and told me the name of the church that he went to. We decided to exchange information so that he can see the scriptures and inspirational messages that I would put on my social network page.

As I got to know him I found out that he was very sweet, and the perfect gentlemen. He attended prayer and bible study at his church and went to church every Sunday. So of course I'm thinking he's the one especially after what I prayed only minutes before I met him. All I needed to do next was find out what line of ministry God called him to and how he was accomplishing the Lords will for his life. I have all these big aspirations and goals that I am going to accomplish for the body of Christ and because it is Gods will. So you know that my spouse and I would have to share the same passion for ministry. When I asked my perfect tall fellow what his spiritual aspirations were he told me he didn't have any. When I asked him if he ever thought about preaching he said no, when I told him that I was going to preach and asked him to come to the service he said that he would see what he could do which ultimately turned into no.

This guy who wanted to take me where ever I wanted to go, whenever I wanted to go there, who was a perfect gentleman would totally shut down when it pertained to him and I in ministry. So I separated myself from him, I told him I didn't have time for what he wanted from me. I wanted to fast and he wanted to eat, I wanted to pray and he wanted to stay on the phone all night, I wanted time to read the Word and he wanted to text all day. It was obvious him and I were in two different categories with our relationship with God.

Soon after I stopped talking to him God began to minister to me about His people. He told me He was not pleased with the amount of divorces, separations and remarriages that happen in the body of Christ. He began to speak to me in detail about what He wanted the single Christian to know before they decided to get into the marriage covenant. Marriage is more than just a piece of paper to God it is a holy, binding union and covenant and building strong Christian marriages starts with strong Christian people. When you are single and living for God you have to work on authentically being the best person you can be according to the gospel.

I believe that God deserves our best before we decide to become one with another person for the rest of our life. If we don't understand how to love God then how can we love another person? Marriage is an honorable union in His eyes and it is not taken as seriously in the Body of Christ as it should be. How do I know that? The divorce rate is too high that's how.

Furthermore, too many highly esteemed preachers and gospel artist break the marriage covenant. This breaks and soils what God said is sacred and what the parties involved vowed to stay in for better or for worse is made void in the eyes of man and then they move on to another marriage or in some cases they move on to other marriages. Even though we see a divorcee, in most cases God sees an adulterer, His Word does not change, and there are no loopholes and ways to compromise with the Word of God. There are no big debates to be made on the topic; the Word is very clear on marriage and what is expected from both parties involved. We have to build ourselves as dedicated to the Lord, His Word and His way while we are single. Honor God with living a holy life now, keep your integrity or faithfulness and dedication as a Christian no matter what and you will honor Him with a Holy marriage later.

Integrity to God is not something developed over night that is why it is important for you to develop it before you are married. Integrity will enable you to be a child of God and carry yourself accordingly at all times no matter what the situation is. Integrity enables you to be receptive to what God says to you and who He has for you. It won't matter how a person makes you feel, or how the person looks if they are not Gods choice for you then you won't want them. Your integrity will not allow you to take the easy way out of marriage however you will exhaust all options and honor your spouse the way the Word of God says you should.

One reason we have become the laughing stock of atheists and unbelievers is because of poor choices before and/or during our marriage, when in all actuality God should be glorified from our unions. People should have a clearer picture of who God is and why we serve Him from the examples set in the holy union of marriage. God gets no glory from these divorces and unions to the wrong people. God operates in order and He expects the same quality in us. Order and integrity in the Lord is just a couple of qualities that should be developed before we join ourselves to another person in holy matrimony. Listen up single Christian, God loves you unconditionally and if you are to marry He wants the best spouse for you. However, God wants you to be the best you that you can be before you meet this person.

In other words, work on developing yourself before you work on developing a relationship, find God before you find a mate. A true love-filled relationship with God will prepare you for marriage. However, any way you look at it God must come first! Strive to be the person who God created you to be so that you can have the spouse that God created you to have. Sometime after God began ministering to me about the single Christian, how displeased He was with the divorce rate for the Body of Christ and how significant the marriage covenant is, my very persistent tall fellow somehow after many unanswered calls and texts got back in contact with me. I was going to give in, I was going to date him I was going to take the relationship as far as it could go since he was so persistent and interested and after all he wasn't that bad...I mean he does go to church and he is 6'4 and handsome.

Just when I made the decision to date him I had a dream. In the dream he and I were together and I was pregnant by him. I had the strangest feeling about my pregnancy and I knew that it would negatively affect the ministry that I had just started at my church as well as my destiny. So I began to ask people that I trusted in my church including my pastor what I should do about my pregnancy. Everyone said the same word over and over ABORT ABORT ABORT.

So that's what I did, I aborted what I was about to birth with this man and my life went back to normal. I felt relieved and at peace with my decision and continued in the Lords will for my life without any negative consequences. When I woke up from this dream I was very troubled and extremely confused as to why everyone would tell me to abort my baby. However the Holy Spirit let me know that the dream was symbolic to what was happening in the natural with my life. I was about to birth a relationship with someone that was going to negatively affect my destiny and my ministry and He wanted me to abort it.

The definition of abort is to bring to a premature end because of a problem or fault and that was definitely the case with this situation. I had to end it early because it was at fault according to the Lord and if it is wrong to God then it is definitely wrong to me; after ending things with the guy for good God put an even greater charge on me to write this book. I've noticed that single Christians have a lot of concerns with dating and for some strange reason even though the Word does not promise us a spouse we spend a lot of time looking for one.

It is of course normal to want companionship, however that is where it should end meaning it is not a desire that we should obsess over.

"God I want a companion, if it is your will for me to have one send them to me at the right time", after saying that feel free to give Him specific details about the qualities you want your spouse to have. God is my best friend, I tell Him everything and at the appropriate times I converse with Him like anyone would converse with a trusted friend. Here is how I view it, He knows it all any way and furthermore He is the only one who can do anything about it. You would greatly benefit from keeping your communication with God open and honest; it will harbor a stronger bond and level of love and trust between you and Him; after we acknowledge our desire for a companion and petition the Lord that should be it.

Our faith and trust in the Lord should tell us that first of all He heard you, and secondly if He has a spouse for you than one day at the right time you will meet them. In the meantime, stay in Gods will, don't be distracted by your desire for a spouse and work on being the most accomplished single Christian you can be. Enjoy this time unshared time with the Lord. Get deep into the Lord and open up yourself to allow Him to get deep into you. There is always a higher level to go with God, there is always more that you can give

Him. So don't ever feel like I've done all I was supposed to do at this point in my life and now I wait for my spouse.

Keep climbing and reaching in God, if He does have a spouse for you, this is a great state of mind for you to continue in after you meet them. For those of you that will not get married it is that same for you, climb, reach and push for your call and destiny in Christ Jesus and continue in this state of mind all the days of your life. I pray that this book illuminates your mind, helps you to grow spiritually and enables you to be the single Christian that God wants you to be.

Simply put, being single means that you are not married. See, when you are not married you don't have a REAL obligation to the person that you are seeing. With just a few words, even if you're engaged, you can tell your partner that you want to call things off and end your relationship. There is nothing binding you to the person that you are with if you are not married. To be frank no matter if you're dating, in a committed relationship or even engaged in Gods eyes you are single until you say "I do".

The engagements nowadays are nothing like the binding betrothal in Jesus' times. For example, if you wanted to break an engagement 2,000 years ago you would have to get a paper of divorce written or you would never be able to marry another person without being considered an adulterer. Today things are completely different culturally and even morally, once you give the ring back it's over. This universal example of what happens when an engagement is broken should prove my point; you were never really attached if all you had to do is give a ring back to rid someone from your life.

Also think about when you fill out paper work and documents, when it comes to your marital status you are either married, single or divorced there is no in between that goes on record concerning your life which further proves my point. In a nutshell if you are not married then you are on the market until someone takes a vow before God saying that you are one with them until death officially taking you off the market! So how does being a Christian effect your relationship status, well for starters you don't give the person that you're dating or who is a prospective lifelong spouse treatment like you are wed.

Today it is the norm for unbelievers to give each other titles like wifey and hubby after dating for about 6 months to a year and to lay things that should be sacred out on the table for their boo. With us Christians we don't play like that, if I am to be your wife/husband I obtain the title once the marriage ceremony is completed. If we as Christians are not married we don't give each other the benefits that unbelievers give each other when they are unwed. It's not normal for us to have children with people that we are not in a marriage covenant with because as believers we know that fornication is a sin and shouldn't happen under any circumstances (1 Corinthians 6:9-10, 18-20 Ephesians 5:3).

As believers we know that we should not live with someone we are in a relationship with unless we are married (1 Corinthians 7:2). You're only human I don't care how Holy Ghost filled you are, to avoid lust and temptation (James 1:13-16) I highly recommend that you and the person you are engaged to live in separate places until you're married. As Christians we should not invest all of our time, bodies and emotions into a person who isn't our husband/wife because they don't deserve it. It is a recipe for disaster, in all things even our relationships God comes first and God is the only One who we should invest all that we have to offer into when we are not married.

Always remember, you are a chosen generation, a royal priesthood, an holy nation, a peculiar people (1 Peter 2:9) and you are to carry yourself as such. With this scripture in mind, consider yourself special you are bought with a price (1 Corinthians 6:20, 7:23), anyone that wants to be in your life has to earn your time and affection you are worth a lot and very precious to God. We are His children and we are to hold ourselves at a high standard at all times. It seems like we as Christians have this ideology that we find Jesus then after we find Him we find love and then marriage then of course comes the babies and we live happily ever after. Ummmm.....why do we believe this? Where in the bible is it even promised that we all are going to get married? It's not there people. The Word of God says "he who finds a wife finds a good thing, and has obtained favor with the Lord (Proverbs 18:22)" because, every man is not promised a wife.

Did a just hear a bubble burst? Ladies, don't you dare go to church scanning every attractive man or man with a title in the church left ring finger. Men don't your dare go to church looking for the woman who has the most ideal physique or child bearing hips and waste time trying to figure out whether she is married to anyone or has children. When you go to church, your only focus should be God and what He is saying to you or through you, there is no room for you to goggle the opposite sex in that equation. Satan will use the opposite sex to throw you off track, yes even in church if you let him.

Have you ever heard of what happened in the Garden of Eden? He will use someone you are sweet on to beguile you in a minute, take you out of Gods will and make your life way more difficult than it has to be. Don't get me wrong church is an exemplary place to meet a spouse, what I am saying is that looking for a spouse should not be one of your main priorities when you’re in the house of God. Women, please stop going out of your way to get a man’s attention when you think he fits the description of the man you want to be with, trust me, you won't have to do backflips for the man who God has for you. He'll find you, just like the scripture says.

Ladies make sure that you carry yourself as a woman of the Most High God should (1 Timothy 2:9-10), modestly! That means you should never be in church or any other place dressed like a wanna be video vixen. Let me be more specific, you know when your shorts are too short, your pants are too tight, your shirt is too low and your dress is too high. The more respect you have for your temple the more respect a man will have for your temple. If your demeanor is that of a woman who is easy then you will attract men who want an easy woman. Treat your body like an earthen vessel with a treasure inside (2 Corinthians 4:7); treat yourself like you house the Holy Spirit. You should not want to present the Light as if it is common. The same goes for you men!

Carry yourselves as mighty men of valor, carry yourself like you were born to be the head of the household. If you want to dress and talk like one of these easily supplanted rappers or entertainers then expect to attract women who are in groupie mode. Pull your pants up, buy your clothes the right size and carry yourself as the king and priest that you are (Revelation 1:6). If you present yourself and talk like you are made in Gods image (Genesis 1:26-27), you will attract women who love God, now doesn't that make sense? Your main objection as Christians should be seeking God, daily spiritual growth and being aligned with whatever the Lords will is for your life. Your quest for God in His fullness has to come before your quest for a spouse, you will not be able to love the right way if you don't love God the right way (1 John 4:7).

The right way to love God is with all of your heart, soul and might (Deuteronomy 6:5). When you understand how to love the Lord, you understand what unconditional love is. Finding out what unconditional love is a scratch on the surface of being ready for marriage because, you are going to have to put unconditional into action every day for the rest of your life. Seeking God first and keeping your focus on Him, will ensure that when you do meet the person that God has for you, you are spiritually mature enough to maintain your growing relationship with Him.

I want you all to keep in mind that marriage is a temporary privilege on earth and in every case no matter what the circumstances are death breaks the marriage covenant. With that being said, marriage is for a little while (Matthew 22:30) however, the relationship you have with God is an eternal one that will not be broken and it should always take precedence over all of your other relationships. Uphold yourself as the righteousness of God through Jesus Christ seek Him diligently and you will be rewarded with what the Lord sees fit for you to have, you have to trust that He knows what is best for you. So kick out the idea that with your salvation comes a spouse, a house with a white picket fence and some children and embrace that the promise of salvation is that you are joint-heirs with Christ and have obtained the gift of eternal life (Romans 8:17). It doesn't get any better than that!

Okay, so now you understand your relationship status and you would like to meet people and get to know them. A recent study of 11,000 people revealed that meeting through mutual friends came in at number two for the top ways to meet your significant other. Meeting at work or school came in at number one, which makes sense. When meeting someone at work you are guaranteed to deal with someone who has some type of (hopefully great) work ethic.

If you are a student you are meeting someone who is taking the responsible route of securing their future with an education. In both instances you are able to get a good look at this person daily to see what type of man/woman you'd be dealing with. It is a pressure free way to get to know someone. In most cases you are both at the same juncture in your lives and can relate to each other, give support to each other and have at least this one thing as a common ground between you two. Just make sure you keep your intentions good and your integrity as a Christian. No one wants an uncomfortable environment at work or at school so be smart and take your time when choosing someone from either place. At number two we have mutual friends. Well, meeting someone through your friends is a great idea depending on the type of friend in question. Is it your "I'm not saved but I respect your lifestyle" friend or is it your "Holy Ghost filled" friend?

The people you surround yourself with have everything to do with the people you attract. If you are always around your unsaved (not living according to the Word, commandments and ways of God) friends then expect to attract unsaved people. If you are always around your saved (living according to the Word, commandments and ways of God) friends than expect to attract saved people. For me personally, if we are not on the same level spiritually than there is only so much of a friend we can be to each other. You want to sing the latest hip-hop song, I don't want to hear that mess, you want to talk about what you and your boyfriend/girlfriend did last night, I don't want to hear that mess, you want to go to clubs and bars and I don't want to be around that mess.

The Word says how can two walk together except they agree (Amos 3:3)? Such a good question, here is the answer YOU CAN'T! If I'm always trying to go right and you are constantly going left where is the agreeance? Don't you know that friendship with the world is enmity with God (James 4:4)? If you are truly saved and can tolerate sin enough to hang around it, party around it and be happy and comfortable around it then something is terribly wrong and you need to be at the next altar call. God does not tolerate sin around Him and we are to be holy as He is Holy (1 Peter 1:16). So how can we truly say we are Christ like if we sit around sinners comfortably and call them our friends? We can't. If you do have unsaved friends, then I highly suggest that you change the people and things that you surround yourself with. Share Christ with them and if they don't accept Him the way that they should, which is by keeping His Word, than shake the dust off of your feet and keep it moving (Matthew 10:14) or in other words leave them alone, be completely done with them and take no part of them with you!! If according to the gospel you cannot be friends with them, then you should know that you definitely cannot let them pick your next date. You both live two different lives, so what they think is okay you think is wrong. You are the righteousness of God through Jesus Christ, do not be unequally yoked with unbelievers (1 Corinthians 6:14) and certainly do not let them pick a spouse for you!!

By now you should either be making a mental note of who needs to be out of your life and who you need to witness to, or patting yourself on the back for having friends who truly love the Lord. Those friends who truly love the Lord should be the friends that you call when you need to hear some Holy Ghost inspired advice. I have a friend who is a minister and whenever I really need some advice pertaining to life, ministry or the Word I message him because he is a true man of God and I know that God will use his mouth to tell me what I need to hear. I had a co-worker who was a true worshiper of the Lord and when she and I sat down to have a conversation we fed each other's spirit, our conversation was always one that gave reverence and glory to the Lord.

I pray that the people that you choose to surround yourself with add positivity and a little more of Gods Spirit to your life. Keep the people who love the God you live for close to you and keep the ones who live for themselves at a distance. What communion hath light with darkness (2 Corinthian 6:14-18)? In your walk with God you are supposed to make the choice to come out from among sinners and be separate from them, you both serve two different Gods and the god they serve is a god with the little g. If you are comfortable hanging out and being friends with people who live a lifestyle opposite to yours, than you will be comfortable dating people whose lifestyle is completely opposite from yours and from one child of God to another let me tell you, that is a huge NO-NO. If your whole life is based upon the doctrine of God, where does a person who doesn't live for Him fit into your life? The people who you call friends tell allot about who you are and where you are spiritually (Proverbs 13:20). Let me give you a clear outline of what I mean. Let's say you just so happen to meet this wonderful saved Holy Ghost filled fire baptized person, they fancy you and you fancy them. They live completely according to the Word of God and are living in Gods will for their life.

It comes time for the person you are sweet on to meet your friends, you all go out to dinner. Your friends are cursing, drinking liquor, and talking about other folks in the restaurant and acting every way but holy. How do you think your prospective spouse will feel about you when dinner is over? I'll tell you how, like you have poor judgment, you are weak in the spirit and somewhere on the inside you are like the people whom you call your friends and felt comfortable with him/her meeting. I know you've heard the saying "birds of a feather flock together", it is not a biblical saying but it is very true.

I've never heard the rich to hang out with the poor and I've never seen prisoners hanging out with the correction officers or homeless people going out for coffee with home owners, so of course it doesn't make sense for saints to hang out and be friends with sinners. Do you see how as a Christian or anyone for that matter, the people you are friends with shows other people who you are and what is acceptable to you and what isn't acceptable? Stay away from forming any type of relationships with unbelievers that you are not trying to draw to Christ.

Now you should all know that I am all for your truly saved friends introducing you to someone to date. You may consider me biased but hear me out; another saved person is literally your brother or sister in the Lord. Their basically like family, don't you know that the blood of Jesus makes you closer to your brothers and sisters in Christ than flesh blood relation? The relationship that you have with them is another thing that will carry on into the other side. Maybe not so much the personal aspect of it but definitely the principle and concept of loving Gods people the way that He does.

Also, your Christian brothers and sisters know firsthand what it feels like to be single and if they are living according to the Word of God they should also be able to make basic judgment calls that would affect your life positively. An example of a basic judgment call is simply, based on what I know about God and His Word would this person be a good match for my brother or sister in the Lord. Remember the example I gave a little while ago about someone you are sweet on meeting your unsaved friends? Let's use the same scenario and make one change, your friends are saved. So it is time for your new Holy Ghost filled honey to meet your friends, you all meet up at a restaurant. Every person at the table is a child of God, no one is drinking alcohol, no one is using foul language and everyone is having a great conversation; a conversation that is edifying that you all can laugh at and learn from, a conversation that is seasoned with salt (Colossians 4:6).

The new person in your life will be comfortable with you and trust you even more for choosing to be friends with people that really uphold the righteous image of God. It will show them how spiritually mature you are and it will also reveal the type of person you are, a person who associates with likeminded individuals who serve God by not just saying they do but actually showing it by their actions (James 1:22). Way better opinion of you right? Now ask yourself, what type of people do I surround myself with? If I were to meet the "right one" tomorrow what type of environment or social circle would I be bringing them into? Your "circle"; whether its family or friends, matters when you are dating and more importantly it will matter when you are married. Keep quality people in your life to avoid certain issues, drama, meaningless situations and conversations. You keep the righteousness of God around you and you cannot go wrong. You can trust that if they are to introduce you to someone, they will be a person after Gods own heart.

Just so there aren't any loopholes and to cover all the basis of this topic, I will write this and be brief and to the point. Even if you do not want your friends to introduce you to someone, as a Christian and based on the scriptures previously sited you still have the same obligation to surround yourself with people who love the Lord like you do. Not because I said so but because the Word says so.

Furthermore, if you are ready to date and choose a mate, you should at the very least be able to successfully choose the correct friends. So when you are with your friends, what do you like to do together? Or what do you like to do when you are not with your friends? The "what do you like to do" question has to be one of the most important questions that someone can ask you when you are getting to know them. Me personally, I like to keep things simple so the theater, a unique restaurant or a museum just about completes my list of what I like to do.

Let me make some suggestions on what should not be on your list of do's anymore since you are a follower of Christ, hip-hop and R & B (or any other type of music that promotes things that are against the God that you serve) concerts, clubs and bars because the people in these places are there to party, get drunk, hook up with the cutest person there or whoever gives them the time of day, listen to music that is everything but holy and they are in there doing things that are not of God. Why would you want to be in that environment? There is no such thing as good or clean fun in the enemy of our soul's territory.

The club and bar scene should simply not be your "thing" anymore as you have passed from darkness to light (1 John 2:8) and have moved on from such worldly things. Okay now, back to that list of what you should not want to do anymore since you are followers of Christ, we already covered types of concerts and bars and clubs. Next on the list is smoking or doing any drug that defiles and potentially damages your body which is the temple of God (1 St. Corinthians 3:16-17), then comes drinking.

The topic of drinking can be a touchy one for some people; it's not for me so I'm going to touch on it. If having a drink is on the list of things that you like to do then you are questionable, there is a difference between having a drink and let me write that one more time A DRINK on occasion and drinking being on the list of things that you like to do. The bible never says drinking is a sin, however we know that the drunkard or the excessive drinker is in sin and will not see the Kingdom of Heaven(1 Corinthians 6:10, Ephesians 5:18, 1 Peter 5:8, Isaiah 28:7, Titus 2:3) and

God takes no pleasure or gets no glory from you drinking too much or too often.

So a drink on occasion is okay, but if every time you get the chance you are ordering or having a drink, you need to take heed and check yourself. Now I know the scripture says a little wine is good for the belly (1 Timothy 5:23) however, that just speaks to the fact that the water in some places thousands of years ago was contaminated and the population had to drink a little wine from time to time so that they would not become ill so frequently.

So you can't use that scripture as an excuse to drink because we have fully functioning water systems that cleanse our water and if your city reservoir is not good enough for you there is always water store brought filters, bottled water, juices, sodas, smoothies, you name it! You can practically juice anything nowadays. Basically if your drinking alcohol it is because you have the desire to, it's not because the bible tells you to. To be quite frank, you are not portraying the appropriate image of Christ if you feel the need to drink when you socialize. This would mean that every time family or friends see you out, you just have to order a cocktail. Someone may be looking at you and your standard of holiness so they'll have a better idea of how to be Christ like. Bear the infirmities of the weaker brethren or babes in Christ (1 Corinthians 8:9, Romans 14:21, Galatians 5:13) and order yourself a virgin Pina Colada or one of those jazzy Shirley Temples. I personally do not drink at all; I like to be of a sober mind. I never know when God wants me to give a message to someone or pray for a person, this has happened and can happen at any given time and I want to be ready at all times no matter if I am hanging out with friends or spending time with family. The work of the Lord always comes first so I have made the choice to always be composed, perceptive and of a clear mind because working for God is a 24 hours a day 7 days a week job.

By now you may be asking yourself why I am spending so much time advocating for a certain lifestyle and imploring you to take certain things off of your "I like to do" list. It is because, as a single Christian who wants to wed, you are preparing for marriage and guess what....marriage is a ministry. Your marriage is a ministry in that it should positively affect the Body of Christ; God does not want you to get married *just* for love. We can love our pets but that doesn't mean that we should marry them.

God wants your marriage to have an equal amount of love and purpose, so this means that your marriage should be a blessing to you and the church. Just like any ministry you have to prepare for it, a person doesn't just up and become an evangelist while they are still clubbing, getting drunk and hanging out with just anybody. They have to stop those things and become a completely new creature in Christ (2 Corinthians 5:18) if they want to have the okay from God to move forward in their calling, and have a blessed and prosperous ministry. It is the same concept with marriage.

As a child of God you cannot go into covenant with Him and another person if you are not living a holy lifestyle. You seek the Kingdom of God first and His righteousness and all these things will be added unto you. In other words, seek God in the fullness of who He is, live according to the gospel and Gods righteous nature and then things will begin to fall into place, remember He is a rewarder of those who diligently seek Him (Matthew 6:33, Hebrews 11:6). You have to make sure you are on the right path with the Lord and that you are all you can be for Him and for yourself before you can become one with another person.

There is not another person who can complete you, change you, fix you or help you the way that the God will. One of your many goals as a Christian should be complete happiness with God, regardless of who is in your life. We stand at the judgment seat of God by ourselves that signifies that our relationship with Him is personal and never has to do with another person being involved in it. Seek Him first, so if marriage or any other ministries are in your future you will be the best person you can be for your assignments. This subject leads us right into my next topic, have you given your all to God? You are a Christian; do you feel like there is some slack on your part? This is the perfect time for you to be honest with yourself. God's desire for you is that you are holy as He is Holy and your ways align with His righteous ways. Once your nature is aligned with who God is, then your desires will be aligned with His will.

So if you are to be married walk in your purpose in earth and you will meet the person who God has for you whenever God deems it the right time and if you are not to be married your life will go the way God wants it to and your purpose will be fulfilled either way. As a single Christian, you are to be the best follower of God you can be! He should be your main priority as you are not obligated to tend to the needs of a spouse. I petition you to sedulously seek the face of God, fast, pray, study His Word consistently and develop an intimate relationship with Him. All this with the expectations of being the spiritual giant God created you to be and getting to know Him in ways you never thought possible.

God has doors that He wants to open for you, but you have to be completely sold out for Him. This is because, if you are not really ready you'll walk into this new door while you are looking back and peeking into other doors that were supposed to be shut forever. Trust God and give all of your heart, soul and power to Him (Deuteronomy 6:5), He has never failed to do exceeding abundantly above all that we could ask or think (Ephesians 3:20). He has the best plans for you (Jeremiah 29:11) and He can and will do better with your talents, gifts and anointing than you can. Allow Him to shape you and mold you (Isaiah 64:8), He will make an impressive specimen out of you and a stunningly inspiring resume for you.

Speaking of resumes, have you looked at your requirements for a spouse and compared them with your accomplishments? Ask yourself, what do I bring to the table besides an alluringly somatic visage? Are you financially stable, do you have short term and long term goals, can you support a household, do you practice saving, how can you cause a surge in the life of your potential spouse? There are so many other questions that you should ask yourself before you decide you want to get married. Often times we think about and focus on what qualities we as individuals want in our spouse, without ever seriously taking into consideration what our future spouse wants. We want this person who has it all together, well, wouldn't it make sense that if they have allot going for them that they would want someone who has allot going for themselves too.

You owe it to God, yourself and this person that you'll one day marry to fulfill your life goals. If you want a car or a house, greater preaching ability, deeper knowledge of the bible, whatever it is, go for it! Do not wait to meet the ideal person and say we will grow together, all the while you are stagnant or doing the basics and bare minimums of life. If and when you do meet the right one, you want them to see all the qualities that they sought in their life long mate. Of course after becoming one with each other, you continue to grow and do remarkable together.

However, growth begins before marriage. You should grow daily and seek greatness with the Lord no matter who is or is not in your life. Listen single Christian, you may never meet a wife/husband, and however you have the Lord always and forever. Keeping, growing and seeking new ways to spice up your relationship with God and being a positive addition to the body of Christ should truthfully always be your top priority.

Nevertheless, supposing that one day you may meet your spouse, what qualities are you hoping to find in them? This is more time of reflection, what are your standards? There are two sides to a person's standards. One side is qualities that are inside of the person and the other side is what they have accomplished in their life. Are you focusing on the most important qualities? The important qualities are qualities that you'll require your spouse to maintain for life. For example, you are going to need your spouse to willingly maintain their love for God and growing relationship with God throughout the rest of your lives together.

You are going to need your spouse to support and help you with the decisions that you make and your obligations to ministry throughout the rest of your life. See where I'm going with this topic of standards? Did you think I was talking about material and physical standards like he/she has to have a Range Rover and work a cool six figure job, for the ladies he has to be at least 6'5 and for the men she has to have hair down to her rare end? No honey, not even a little bit, those things can disappear in an instant. I am not saying attraction is not important, because it is.

However, attraction should not be a deciding factor in whether you marry a person or not. If they have all the qualities that you want in a spouse and they do not meet your physical requirements, this person still deserves a chance. There are a lot of important things that your marriage will require and looks is not anywhere on the list of those things. I would love to marry a man who is 7 feet tall and three hundred pounds of pure solid muscle, smooth silky skin and beautiful pearl white teeth so bright that when he smiles I swoon.

However, if I meet a man of God is 5'5 one hundred and fifty pounds with a few blemishes on his skin who meets all the important requirements, I would be privileged to date and possibly build a relationship with him. So when I speak of standards, looks are not what I have in mind. What I am talking about is the person's heart, dedication, acclaim, ambition, safeguarding, perseverance and appreciation that they will keep for God, you, their ministry, your ministry and their family. I am talking about priceless things that you cannot buy.

With this being said, there are two important parts to the standards that you have for your mate. One side which in my opinion is the most important side is what I just went over, the qualities that you cannot configure. These qualities are a part of a person's soul, they stem from the inside. The second part is this person's accomplishment so far in life as well as their long term and short term goals. You have a couple of Master Degrees, so you want someone with a Doctorate, you have a house and in turn you want someone with a house. You own your own business so ideally you want to be with an entrepreneur.

I personally think that is wonderful, I don't think there is anything wrong with having high standards for who you decide to become one with. It is however imperative that you understand you cannot have one side of your standards without the other. If you have a well accomplished prospective who could care less about what you are passionate about, or doesn't share a deep love for the Lord, they are not the one. You have to share your whole entire life with this person; they should most definitely be concerned with the things that concern you. Now, as wonderful as you are, you have to know when it is okay to compromise. So they may not have the Doctorate, they have an Associate's Degree and have a deep love for God and His people. They are full of vision, accomplished and support you one hundred percent in whatever your calling may be. Don't you dare let this person go over something as insignificant as they are a couple of degrees short of what your human brain said is perfect! On the flip side, you have someone who has a great passion for ministry, loves the Lord with all their heart and treats you like the king/queen that you are, however they are not financially stable and are not trying to be, they are uneducated and have no desire to further themselves in anything but ministry. What do you do?

My suggestion is that you keep this person as a friend until they mature and develop some type of work ethic or they begin to make steps towards advancing themselves career wise to ensure that they will be an active financial contributor to your household. Now of course if you are married and your spouse loses their job, you pick up the slack without complaining, you both are one and the way that you make sure you are taken care of is the way that you are to support your spouse.

Luckily for you, you are not married yet. Do not intentionally walk into a burdensome relationship. Make smart, sensible and most importantly God glorifying decisions that will ensure that if you and the person you are dating do decide to get married you both will start off your lives together the right way. When it comes to your standards, there has to be a balance. Make sure the person has a genuine love for God as well as an obligation to be an optimum provider your family.

Now let's proceed into the topic of compatibility and compromise. These are two very important words when you are figuring out the type of person you want to spend the rest of your life with. Compatibility means that two things are able to exist together without conflict, so what makes you and your prospective compatible? Compromise means to settle a dispute by mutual concession, what standard(s) will you and/or your prospective have to change to be able to move forward on one accord with each other? I will toss out a few examples for you.

We are both Christians, we are compatible as far as that is concerned. We don't like to argue, we believe it doesn't accomplish anything, however we feel it is best to talk about whatever the issue is and in some cases agree to disagree. That definitely makes you both compatible pertaining to that particular topic. You do not like to argue and you are with someone who does like to argue. How would you both be able to settle differences in a way that is appeasing for you? You won't, one will dominate the discussion and one won't be able to get their point across. In that aspect you are definitely NOT compatible. You are a Christian and your prospective is a Muslim, don't do it! Take it from me, I've dated outside of my religion in the past and it will not work people!

You as Christians are not compatible with anyone that opposes the God you serve. You will have more debates than you can count and your life will be full of discontent simply because the person you chose to link up with does not agree with the center of your life which is Christ. Please keep in mind that dating certain type of people will be a complete waste of time, and marrying them will bring a lifetime of heartache. Remember the person that you choose to be with will not only share a bed with you for the rest of your life, they will also be a parent to your children and have a firm say on how they are raised. Even while you are dating, pay close attention to your possible mate and ask a lot of questions.

Always "soberly" think about the future! Their stubbornness is cute now; will it still be cute in 10 or 20 years? Being compatible with a person with the important things in life is essential because it means that you two are in agreement. How can you begin your life with someone if you both don't agree on what is important (Amos 3:3)? Make sure that you do as this saying and "learn how to have hard discussions". When we date someone, we fall in love and everything feels like cotton candy, sunshine and fields of orchids. We don't think about what really matters because we become so adrift in our feelings, that our feelings are all that matters.

When in actuality, once you fall in love with someone you need to anchor yourself in reality. It is time to discuss consequential matters such as money; how do they feel about it and what are their spending habits, family: what type of family do you have, has your history with them been positive or negative, how orderly or tidy are you: do you know how to keep a clean house, how important is cleanliness to you, children: how many children would you like to have, how do you feel children should be disciplined, health: what type of sicknesses or diseases are common in your family? You may think I am over thinking this compatibility topic, but I am not! Right now, in plenty of homes in America there is a wife picking up a her husband's jeans from the middle of the bedroom floor, a husband whose mother-in-law makes his life miserable, a family who cannot afford to go on vacation together because mommy like to go to Nordstrom's and spend every dime her husband tries to save and a woman who wants to have 4 children only to find out after 5 years of marriage that her husband doesn't want any children at all.

I beseech you people; please talk about the aforementioned topics and any other important topics that you can think of. Be incisive and direct because forever is a long time! If you feel like you can't imagine your life without a person, just think about your life before you met them you were living just fine weren't you? If need be move on to some one that you are compatible with. Remember the guy I told you about in the foreword of this book? Him and I were not compatible because him and I were in two different categories spiritually, yes he was sweet, cute and very tall however, sweet, cute and tall cannot hold an edifying conversation with me about the things that the prophet Ezekiel beheld, or the dreams that the prophet Daniel had. You should know what matters in life are most important to you, and those are the things that should be a common ground for you and your future mate.

So, you don't feel like the person that you are dating is compatible with a lot of the things that are important to you. However, you have feelings for them and you see potential in them, this is when the topic of compromise becomes your recourse. You cannot compromise on the things that are most important to you; your religion is never up for negotiation. So with religion out of the question, what are you willing to compromise to be with this person? I suggest that you never compromise what makes you happy for someone else that you are not obligated to. That would be giving them treatment as if you were espoused to them and that is treatment that they have not earned and do not deserve.

I will give you some examples of what I believe you can compromise your standards for and still be happy. You didn't want to marry a person who has children, however you meet this lovely person who fits the description of exactly who you pictured yourself spending the rest of your life with and they have a child. In this situation it is okay to compromise your standard of wanting to be with someone who has no children as long as the other parent in the equation is not an issue and the person that you are with is a loving, caring provider for their child. Remember, compromising should not only make one person in the relationship happy, both people in the relationship should be satisfied with the decision. Next I will use a personal example, I am a vegetarian and on top of being a vegetarian I don't eat fried food and a lot of other things. I however, am willing to be with a person who eats meat. I can make that compromise, it doesn't affect my happiness and also it doesn't affect my lifestyle.

Keep in mind that the compromise you make with the person in question will follow you for the rest of your life, like my mother always says "you start out how you want to end up". With that being said I am willing to fry chicken for my mate and smother some pork chops, it won't bother me a bit. It comes with the territory of having this person and I accepted it before we got married so now I have to deal with it. So don't ever resent the person for the compromise that you decided to make to be with them, make sure it is something that you can live with forever. Unlike the marriages of unbeliever we are not supposed to get divorced.

Divorce is not supposed to happen with a Christian marriage with the exception of change in religion or adultery and even then if you can reconcile after the incident please do. We as Christians need to start showing the world that we have God and He makes the difference in our marriage and how we handle things. It amazes me how Christians especially Christians in ministry can divorce in remarry in front of their congregation, their brethren and in front of the world like the doctrine we live by makes exceptions for the individual. There are many people standing in the pulpit who are considered adulterers according to the Word of God (Matthew 5:32, 19:9).

Make sure you are not being taught by someone who doesn't value what God values. We as Christians are Christians because we choose to follow the doctrine of Christ, the entire thing. We cannot just take out the parts that are convenient for us; we have to follow the entire Word of God as a whole. This makes our relationship completely different from a mundane relationship.

As a Christian, our relationships are based on different principles than people who live outside of the will of God. It is requisite that our relationship is built on the solid foundation that is Christ and rooted in the principles of God. As a believer we understand that acknowledging and obeying the will of God for our life by living according to it is the only beneficial option for us. We cannot partake in certain activities if they are not pleasing in the sight of God. In this world there are things that should literally repulse or vex us (2 Peter 2:8); we should not in any way try to simulate the ways of the world. We are to be holy and separate and that carries over into the principles of our relationship.

As Christians we have discretion (Proverbs 11:22) with the personal aspects of our relationships and integrity with the person that we are involved with and there are certain things we don't tell people. This builds trust as well as intimacy (non-related to sexual intimacy. This intimacy refers to that of personal time together building familiarity, togetherness and a bond) with each other and keeps the vital things sacred between you two.

Pray together, fast together, study the Word of God together, go to church together when you can, support each other's endeavors and this will be the beginning of not only a tight-knit friendship but also true love and dedication to each other.

These are the principles that a Godly relationship should be built on. It is imperative that you as a Christian put God first in your relationships. If this is a person that you are thinking about spending the rest of your life with, you should begin sharing some of the personal time that you spend with God with your eventual spouse. This means that if you usually fast on Tuesdays, the person you are getting serious with should occasionally fast on Tuesdays with you.

Together and on one accord ask God to bless your relationship, ask Him to make your way straight with this person (Proverbs 3:6), petition God together for each other's individual needs and always put God first! Putting God first is what distinguishes our relationship from a worldly relationship. I understand that you are a Christian and your relationship is not one that is based on the lust of the flesh (1 John 2:16-17) like a worldly one, but that doesn't mean that the sexual aspect of your future marriage has never crossed your mind. So as you are building this tight-knit relationship of trust, love, intimacy and dedication with your eventual spouse, do you ever discuss sexual intimacy? This is definitely a taboo subject however inquiring minds need to touch on this for clarity.

First and foremost being able to discuss the topic of sexual intimacy with your eventual spouse all depends on you and the person that you are with level of maturity. If you both can handle the conversation of sexual intimacy without being filled with lust and inappropriate thoughts, then go for it. I was asked the question by one of my students "why can't we 'do it' before we get married, how am I going to know whether or not I'll like it?" As Christians developing a relationship our love and desire to be with each other is not based on sex it is based on agape love; of course at some point growing into Philia which is a mental love and affection for one another which ultimately becomes Eros a romantic, passionate and physical love shared between two people who are attracted to each other.

However, agape love must come first because it is a spiritual based love that completely subjugates things pertaining to the flesh and we as children of God walk in the Spirit (Galatians 5:16, 17, 25). It is a binding love that cannot be dominated by the things of this world. However, we as humans have this invariable curiosity especially when it pertains to pleasurable things.

This means that some of us will have to discuss sexual intimacy. Let me make this clear, if you discuss the topic of sex with someone I highly suggest it is with a person that you are definitely going to marry. This topic is one that you only want to discuss with someone that you have every reason to believe that you are going to spend the rest of your life with, and after the marriage ceremony engage in coitus. You are precious, wonderful and unparalleled, any and every person that you are dating does not deserve the luxury of having such a personal conversation with you. Only a person that has officially made the proposal of marriage or accepted the proposal of marriage has a legitimate reason for wanting to discuss this subject.

You should not ask anything that will disrespect the person you are engaged to and that will cause you to look perverse. Before you decide to talk about sex, you should ask yourself what is your influence and reason for wanting to discuss it. Is it because you want to know what things you can bring on your honeymoon to spice things up, is it because of curiosity or is it because you need a vivid picture of what could potentially happen. Whatever the reason keep in mind that this topic for most normal human beings, if discussed in an explicit way, in too much detail or for too long, will provoke or awaken thoughts and feelings that need to stay asleep until you are both married.

Either way pump your brakes, ask God to guide you to the right decision with this matter and do an honest self-examination before delving into this topic. In my opinion there are only two questions that are discreet yet overt, you get straight to the point and a straight answer, the person gives you a surfeit amount of information without the embarrassment of giving you details. Are you ready for the perfect questions for this situation? Here they are......once we are married, what you think your sex drive will be on a scale from one through ten. Or, once we are married, as a couple what do you think our level of sexuality will be on a scale from one through ten? They may say three, they may say one million, whatever the response is, and it should quench your curiosity for the subject.

Whatever the answer is the scale should give you a clear idea of what you'll be dealing with and everything else you want to know can be discovered and discussed after you are married. Single Christian please hearken to what I am about to say to you. If you ever get married no one can tell you how to carry yourself in the bedroom with your spouse. It is something personal and private. Now more than ever, I am seeing Christian marriage seminars that are supposed to spice up the sex life of the Christian married couple. In my opinion there is a very worldly and very fleshy rationale behind this new trend. Sex is a sacred and personal act between a husband and his wife, when did it become okay for someone to sell tickets for you to sit in their sanctuary and advise you on the one thing that is truly no one else's business but your own.

The fact of the matter is... sex is the only thing in your life that is completely between you and your spouse. You do not have the need to invite anyone else or their opinions into your bedroom. As one, you both should be able to come together and figure the sexual aspect of your life out. You are an individual couple and your needs and ways are different from the next marriage, when did they start giving out licenses for pastors and their partners or anyone else in ministry to dictate or suggest how things are done sexually between a husband and wife? If you can't find common ground with your sex life, you both have to work on communication and listening skills.

If you take my advice and build open communication with each other from the time that you begin dating, communication in marriage will not be an issue. Dating is not the time to forge the exterior of what you think the person you are with wants, it is time to be yourself. I am sure that you expect the same thing from the person you are dating; it is only fair for both parties to know exactly what they will be signing up for in the long run. Am I saying bear it all to them during the first date? Absolutely not, what I am saying is always be yourself and stay true to who you are and communication will not be an issue.

What I am about to do is going to save you and your eventual spouse some money so in the future instead of buying two marriage sex seminar tickets, take your boo out to dinner. Okay I am going to assume that you have your bible, turn with me to Hebrews chapter thirteen and verse four. See there! I am going to translate that for you; God is fine with and is not judging what goes on in the bedroom between two married people with each other. So, looking ahead you both can experiment with each other and try different things which is good to do as time goes on to keep things exciting and new.

You don't have to worry about something in the bedroom not being "Christian" because as long as you are married your sex life is with honor and undefiled in the eyes of God. So if anyone on this planet has the right to be a "freak" it is only a married couple. Just remember to keep whatever goes on between you two to yourselves, when people look at you, you want them to see Christ and nothing else. The personal aspect of your marriage should remain unknown to everyone, in this matter be territorial! Whatever your spouse has to offer is yours and only yours and nobody has the right to know about your goodies.

Remember this when it comes to personal matters, Christians should always be classy, discreet and make wise choices. So if you must talk with your brothers and sisters in Christ about your relationship no matter where the conversation may go make sure you always keep it classy, discreet and wise. So when you do get married have fun the way you want to, if you need help or new ideas research things with each other but do not allow another person into your bedroom ever!

So how long do you wait before you know for sure that this is the person that you want to marry? In my opinion, after a year or a year and a half of consistently getting to know someone, dating and building your relationship with them you should definitely know whether or not you want to spend the rest of your life with them. If you are not sure, I suggest dating other people because maybe this person does not possess the qualities that you want in someone you are going to spend the rest of your life with.

I also suggest instead of dating other people take a break from dating and focus on the qualities that you want in a person. It is hard for us to make those decisions when we are dating because we find ourselves compromising our preferred qualities in a spouse to fit this one person that we are with when in all actuality we don't have to compromise anything! Remember you are not married so you are not obligated to compromise at this phase in your life. Our God does not want us confused and He sure does not want us to settle when it comes to making a decision on who we will spend the rest of our life with, our Father does not want you going into covenant with just anybody.

Pray and search yourself, too much compromise in the long run will leave you feeling void and unfulfilled and after the "I do's" it is too late for you to be uncertain. If you are not sure about the person you are seeing decelerate, possibly date other people and weigh your options and never let anyone force you into a relationship prematurely or into a relationship that you do not want. In twelve to eighteen full months, you talk to someone daily, you go out with them at least once a week, you go to church together from time to time, you pray together, fast together and study the bible together, you hang out and have fun together, you should know whether or not you want to move forward into something more serious with this person.

Personally, I am not one to waste my time or anyone else's, if we do not know how we feel about moving forward with our relationship after about a year then it would probably be best if we remained close friends and moved on to other prospective. Just because you know you want to marry a person, that does not mean that you have to start planning the wedding right away. It just means that you both are clear on what you are doing with each other and the changes that are going to happen moving forward in your relationship.

Once you both figure out you are serious about each other, you may want to start meeting each other's families, church families and friends. This makes the statement to everyone that you are both exclusively involved and you have to begin to build some type of rapport with the people who are close to the person you are dating; eventually they will be close to you also. Again I say it is always important to keep open communication with whomever you are dating or in a relationship with. This is because, you both want to be on one accord, clear about what is going on with each other and the direction that you both will be moving in together. Before you both jump the broom you may want to make sure that this is definitely without a doubt Gods choice for you. The only way to do that is through prayer, ask God to give you a sign (Isaiah 7:11, 7:14, Judges 6:17).

God will speak to you concerning your life, in prayer, through His Word, His prophets, a situation you find yourself in, a dream or He will simply and literally speak to you. Make sure that you are ready, receptive and seeking to receive the sign from God. God does not want you to unite or yoke yourself with someone who He does not want you to be with. Please remember to seek God in prayer and meditation before making the life changing decision of marriage.

God will link you to someone that will positively affect your life and the ministry that He has for you. Technically speaking, your whole life as a follower of Christ is being conformed to His image, living according to His Word and being obedient to Him by staying within His will for your life. Gods will for you is your ministry for we know that the Body of Christ is large and has many functions (1 Corinthians 12:14). You may be in music ministry, you may be a preacher, you may be a healer, a prophet, intercessor etc. but whatever your ministry is, it is exactly what God wants it to be and has entrusted you with.

You have to protect and nurture your ministry with your entire being. It matters who you date and if you get married you will become one with this person, how will this union impact the ministry that God has given you. From one believer to another, if you are in ministry whatever your ministry may be you are held at a high standard in the eyes of God. If you are to minister in any way, you have to assure your life is right with God before you come before His people and proclaim the Gospel. Other leaders and your brothers and sisters in the Lord need to know that your life is aligned with the Word that you will be ministering to different congregations and people. Does this person you are dating live a lifestyle that is pleasing to God? Are they half stepping or are they really living for God?

Do they have direction in their life and are they fulfilling their destiny with the Lord? Are they doing the bare minimum for God or are doing all that is in their power? These are question that you need to ask yourself as a Christian. You cannot expect to change a person's salvation status or relationship with God by being in a relationship with them. Be their friend and share the Gospel with them and if they don't personally hearken to the Word of God they most definitely will never genuinely hearken to you spoon feeding the Lord to them. You are not living your life to please other people however; you are a part of a body. Do not attempt to attach a foreign object to the Body and expect it to be accepted and work normally. There is only one way to become a part of the Body of Christ and that way is through Jesus (John 14:6), not you! If you are the anointed and appointed of God make sure that the person you decide to date is too. You are hot for God and if they are cold or warm, you will be a warm union (Revelation 3:16).

When you come together with another believer you both should be on fire for the Lord! Physical attraction is a lovely thing, however it is vain to base the reason you date someone solely on their looks. Remember you are aiming for agape love; not fading love...when the looks fade the love fades with it. When you walk in the Spirit, dating someone because they are attractive can get old very quickly. If you are spiritual you need someone who can cater to the spiritual part of you and a cute face cannot do that. As a person who lives in the Spirit you will need sound Godly counsel, support and conversation from the person you are dating.

When you meet someone that you would potentially like to date, check out their spiritual resume before you decide to give them a shot.

What have they done for the Lord, what are their Spiritual gifts (1 Corinthians 12:3-11), what is their call in ministry (1 Corinthians 12:28), what are their future goals for the Lord. These are questions that whoever you are thinking about dating should have an answer to. When you are one who ministers to the people of God in any way, people look at your lifestyle, sometimes out of admiration and sometimes to get a clear picture of what is acceptable and what is not acceptable.

Make sure that you do not go around dating everyone and anyone, hold yourself at a high standard and keep a high standard for the type of person that you spend your time with. Also, make sure that whoever you choose to date is a positive reflection to other believers of who you are and what is expected from a Christian. Make sure that your relationship is with someone that knows the Word and can assist and encourage you through the things that people who work for the Lord have to go through. Always keep in mind that you want a positive addition to your life and your ministry, not just an attractive appearance. As the called of God you need substance in whoever you are with, whether it's just a platonic friendship or someone you are dating the people in your life should display the same morals and lifestyle as you do. Furthermore, whoever you are dating should be an asset to your life and to your ministry endeavors whenever they can be, considering that they have their own ministry and obligations to attend to. If you are reading this book and you do not have a ministry, think again! God created us all with a purpose, seek Gods will for your life through prayer, meditation and fasting. While you are figuring out what you are called to do, keep yourself busy by studying the Word of God and helping out at your church in any way that you can. God is all for you and there is nothing stopping you from getting busy for the Lord. Now back to the original topic of how your relationships affect your ministry.

God also wants you to associate yourself with people who are in your category. This person should feed your spirit by engaging you in edifying conversations from time to time, this is an essential quality needed in a spouse for those of you who walk in the Spirit. Everything does not have to be "deep" all of the time however when it is time to get "deep" whoever you are dating should be able to take you there. If a person seems to meet all of the necessary criteria to be with such a great person as yourself, then comes this question, can you see yourself with them every day for the rest of your life? Can you see the both of you building something solid together in the future? Will they be an excellent parent, is this the person that you want to bring children into this world with and see every morning when you wake up?

Are you willing to grow with them, help them, minister to them, encourage them, share with them no matter what the circumstances are, as long as you both live? Taking into consideration the aforementioned things about the standards you have for yourself combined with these questions, if you answered yes to everything then you may be ready to move forward in to something official and lasting with this prospective spouse. I also suggest that you take in to consideration that, just because a person is saved, you both have a lot in common and you get along great doesn't necessarily make them "the one". Dedicate time to a person to get to know them and do not mistake someone who is a platonic friend for someone that you should date. Ladies, seek out Gods will for your life and if you know in your heart that apart of Gods will is that you get married ask Him to send the person when you are ready. I do not advocate for ladies to go out as an aggressor and push up on every man that has good qualities, I believe it is unbecoming. You do not want to be the female that is in every attractive man's face at church trying to get their contact information. Trust that God will put the right man in your path at the right time and things will fall in to place in a decent orderly fashion (1 Corinthians 14:40).

Men of God seek Gods will for your life and if it is His will that you are to be married then ask Him to allow you to meet the woman He has set apart for you at the right time, when you are ready. It is also unbecoming as a man of God to flirt and try to get to know every woman that matches your criteria. Ask for discernment with all things including this matter. Believe that when it is the right time, God will say "she is the one". While you are waiting for "the one", I think that it is completely fine to date; I just don't think its fine to date everybody.

When you do meet your future spouse, you don't want them to know you as someone who has dated many people. Dating too many people while you are single makes you seem immature and ambivalent, I mean come on you thought ALL these people were worth your time? Remember, keep a high standard for yourself, not everyone is worth your time. Let's touch on the topic of how to carry ourselves as we date. I believe it is a rather simple topic, be yourself and constantly maintain your holiness. I personally do not think it is okay while you are dating a person to kiss (make-out), cuddle and/or engage in any type of "heavy petting" with them. Man, you do that and in my opinion you are knocking on the doors of lust fornication. Stay away from all things that stem from lustful feelings.

I know most people would beg to differ and cannot see the harm in kissing or even cuddling. Listen, everyone is different and it all depends on you and the person that you are dating level of control. I will not be kissing anyone until after I am married, the act of kissing seems very intimate and I happen to believe that my lips should be preserved for my marriage partner. I mean, am I going to kiss everyone that I date? Most of the time when you are dating someone it is uncertain if they are the person that you are going to marry, so that leaves the burning question...what am I kissing them for? What are the feelings that are leading me to kiss them based on? Is it love or lust.

Oh and thinking that a kiss will help determine whether this person is "the one" or not is complete rubbish. Your knowledge of whether a person is the one that you are going to pursue a lifetime with has to be based on a lot more than a kiss; that tingly feeling that you get when you kiss....just about any person that you kiss and are attracted to can give you that feeling. Do not let your flesh deceive you, walk in the spirit, use God and discernment when making life changing decisions. You also do not want to develop romantic feelings with someone solely based on the emotions you experience when you kiss or cuddle with them because those feelings are temporal and can potentially fade.

Your relationship has to founded on a more solid foundation. Remember your goal with this person is agape love, kissing and any other type of romantic intimacy before marriage has nothing to do with developing agape love. However, it does have a lot to do with satisfying your flesh. As far as I am concerned, my lips and body are all too precious and every person I date does not deserve to kiss me or cuddle with me or do anything else that can invade my personal space for that matter. Keep yourself preserved so that when you finally do kiss and cuddle with your spouse, it will feel intense and extra special. I believe that you are worth the wait and you should too. A kiss on the cheek or a hug is harmless.

I beseech you to know where to draw the line, too much intimacy too soon denotes us making decisions based on the wrong emotions. Be of a sober mind when you make the choice to further your relationship with someone, lust and the wrong type of romance will definitely cloud your judgment. The wrong romance before marriage is the things previously mentioned like kissing, touching, feeling or cuddling. The right type of romance is walks in the park, roses, gifts and picnics. Aspire for the right type of romance for your relationship; the right romance will evolve your feelings of agape love to genuine Philia and Eros. The right type of romance is what is appropriate for Christian people who are not yet married. You want God to get the glory out of the way you handle situations, carry yourself and the decisions that you make.

So now, let us move on to another very important topic, divorce and working through the changes that we as humans go through. I pray that you have a happy, God-filled, successful marriage and never have to experience divorce. Also, after everything you have read in the bible and in this book about divorce, it really should never be an option for you and your spouse. Yes, as time progresses people change and if this person that you are married to changes you should be right there with the precise support that they need for whatever their transition happens to be. How many of us can say that we are the same person today as we were five years ago? Hopefully none of us can say that. Change is natural and even though it would be nice if change were always positive, it is not always positive. Sometimes it is negative. The type of love we have as Christians is unconditional love, and with that type of love comes obligations.

You are obligated or bound to your spouse, whether they change for the better or for the worse. So your wife used to watch sports with you all the time, however for some reason two years into the marriage she is not a sports fan anymore. Do you love her any less? Of course not, respect her feelings and opinion and from now on watch sports alone. These situations are perfect for adding extra spice to your marriage. If you cannot share quality time watching sports together anymore, begin to think of something new that you both can do together and enjoy. No more football season with your wife on the couch eating hoagies means that the old routine can be substituted with can be substituted with new a membership to a sports center and do some indoor rock climbing or stay in and during football season she plays offense and you play defense.

Make sure to enjoy your spouse in every way possible regardless of how they change. Always be willing to compromise in marriage and remember that spending quality time together and having fun with each other is crucial. Okay now here's one for the ladies, your husband for the first ten years of your marriage would paint your toes every Saturday night. Now, out of the clear blue sky, he decides he doesn't want to do any more pedicures. Do you start an argument over this? Of course not! Paint your own toes and from time to time you should even ask his opinion on what color nail polish you should use. This person is one with you and a lot of changes that happen concerning personality and desires are usually changes that we can find a happy medium with if we stop being so self-absorbed and communicate with each other.

Here is one last example that gives both sexes food for thought. Your spouse begins to gain weight, 5 years into the marriage they are one hundred pounds heavier. Is this divorce worthy? Do you decide to sleep in the guest bedroom now? Are you going to stop going out to dinner with them? No, no and no! Remember earlier in the book we talked about physical attraction not being enough to base whether or not this person is the one you will spend the rest of your life with? Now do you see what I mean, God is not going to care that you didn't find your spouse sexy anymore so you no longer wanted to have sex with them. The Word says render unto your spouse due benevolence (1 Corinthians 7:3-4) and nowhere in the text was there an *except* if you do not find them attractive anymore. This is one of many reasons why it is important to have a marriage that is built in foundations of real love.

Remember agape of course comes first, then Philia and then Eros. By the time you develop the romantic love of Eros, this person will be attractive to you because of your deep love for them and all the qualities that they possess. So in marriage whether they gain twenty pounds or one hundred pounds, when you look at them you will always see the love of your life and nothing can change that. Also, in such cases, you still have to be there and support them. Start eating healthier to encourage them to get down to a healthier size, take walks together or join a gym, compromise and make it work.

What I am saying is, there is no reason to stop "loving" your spouse or being the spouse that you vowed to be besides adultery. Even though all cases of adultery can end your marriage, they should not, if you can reconcile and continue into a healthy marriage then please do. God gets no pleasure or glory when two Christians divorce each other. One huge and essential quality of God is His faithfulness to us, even when we are not faithful to Him and stays by our side and does everything in His power to reconcile us to Him, not just out of obligation, not with un-forgiveness and bitterness but with loving-kindness He draws us back to Him.

Remember this if God forbid your marriage faces tough times. So divorce should not be an option for you single Christian if both parties are dedicated and faithful to the marriage. Now let's speak about dating a person who is divorced. Is it okay? Well, under a couple of very specific circumstances it is okay to date, build a relationship with and even marry a person who is divorced. There are two reasons that make it acceptable to date or marry a divorced person without being an adulterer. The first reason is found in 1 Corinthians chapter 7 verse 15.

If the person that you are considering a prospective is divorced because they had a spouse who was an unbeliever and this spouse chose to leave them, you can date them. The bible is very clear; it says a person is not under bondage in such cases. So that means they are not bound to the person anymore, God wants His people to have peace and if their unbelieving spouse left them, they are freed from their marriage. Being free from their marriage and not bound by the vows anymore, this person is free to move on in peace. The other reason is the most popular reason, adultery. In Matthew chapter 5 verse 32 Jesus Christ our Savior states that whoever divorces their spouse, unless it is because of infidelity in the marriage, they and whoever they marry is committing adultery.

So if you do decide to date someone who is divorced please ask them the question of how their marriage ended. I understand that it is a personal question and maybe even a little uncomfortable. Remember earlier in the book when I said that you have to "have hard conversations" sometimes? Well, this would be one of those hard conversations. Furthermore, I am sure you would rather ask them and be straightforward in the beginning before you think about a relationship with a person who could potentially make you an adulterer. Believe me there are no loopholes in the Word of God (Luke16:17), it says exactly what it means especially when it comes to Gods standards for us.

So take the Word of God for what it is worth and please take it seriously. There are no exceptions for anyone's individual situation. So unless the person was divorced for one of the two aforementioned reasons, run the other way!

One major thing that we as single Christians struggle with is peace of mind as we wait for the spouse that God has for us. God why do I have to wait so long? God where is my happy ending? God why did you allow me to go into a marriage that would end in divorce? God why did you create me with needs but not give me anyone to meet them? We bombard heaven with countless questions daily concerning our relationship status and our feelings about being single. It amazes me that we have been given the privilege to know the Creator of the universe, who promised to never leave us nor forsake, personally and choose to complain to Him about not having someone who we don't even know yet. We spend time with Him praying and wondering what His plans are for our future concerning a spouse when He heard you the first time you prayed about it. If we prayed for spiritual gifts and greater communion with God as much as we did for a spouse the Body of Christ would be, in this day and age, known for raising the dead and healing the sick. We know that it is possible but the world doesn't....maybe because we aren't compelling enough.

What I'm saying is that there is a lot of work to do for the Kingdom of God; waiting should not be an issue. If we focused on being powerful single Christians, when the time comes we would definitely be powerful married Christians. We have this subconscious mindset of entitlement when it comes to marriage, we feel like it comes with this package called life and salvation. I want you to ask yourself, does not having a spouse hinder your happiness? Well in the Lord there is fullness of joy, so if you aren't happy you need to go deeper in God. The Word says in Psalm 16:11 in God's presence there is fullness of Joy and pleasures at His right hand forevermore. This means that your joy and pleasures should come from being in the presence of God and this joy and pleasure lasts forever! The Word does not say that in marriage there is fullness of joy and everlasting pleasures.

The joy and pleasure of marital bliss is temporary, which means it can come and go. There is no human being on this earth that has the power to provide you with fullness of joy and eternal pleasure, so if we are lacking joy and pleasure in our life we need to spend more time in the presence of God. No human was meant to fill these voids that we have in life, God is the only One capable and willing to be our everything and supply us with the things that we lack spiritually and emotionally. So looking for happiness from a person is like eating cake when you're hungry, it looks good, it's sweet and tastes delicious however it cannot and is not meant to sustain you. On the other hand, looking for happiness in God is like eating a home cooked meal; not only are you full; you are satisfied and peaceful enough to rest.

See, the cake comes after you have eaten the meal, just like your spouse comes after you've ingested the Lord into yourself. As a single Christian you have to be one with God before you *want* to be one with another person. Being one with the Lord requires you to be on one accord with Him, so if God wants you to wait then you should want to wait. Food for thought: two happy people make a better marriage than two people who need each other to be happy, two spiritual people make a better marriage than two people who need each other to be spiritual. Better yourself on purpose; think of things that you can do that will make you an outstanding single Christian who God will be proud of. Getting busy gives your mind less time to wonder onto the topic of relationships and builds you and the Kingdom of God, so using your time wisely is a win win situation for you.

When we have too much free time we tend to have idle thoughts or do insignificant things. We began to talk to that ex, hang out in scenes we stayed away from or entertain thoughts that we used to rebuke. What we allow in our lives shows God exactly what we are ready for, if you still have dealings with a pass that God has removed you from than you can't possibly be ready for the future. Keep your eyes forward; focus on your future and what you can presently do to build it. Right now get a piece of paper and make a list of things you can do to make the best possible life for yourself and do not include a spouse however make sure to include God.

Now get a game plan and get busy, waiting isn't really "waiting" if you are focused on other things. When you possibly meet your future spouse, do you "A" just want to be waiting for them, or "B" do you want to be building your life while enjoying it. I sure know which of those options would make the better impression on your prospective. If you don't, it's option B. It is very desirable to be with a person who is building, living and enjoying their life, not for another person but just because they love themselves enough to secure their future while enjoying their present. You have to choose which person you want to be, the waiter or the mover. I chose to be the mover, I chose to dream big and accomplish everything that I set my heart to do. I chose to enjoy my life and not "wait".

I chose to perceive each and every second of life on this earth as precious, too precious to wait to enjoy with another person when I have the Lord on my side. I chose to be the best single Christian possible, whether I have a "soul mate" or not. I chose to fall in love with God, wrap myself in His presence and get lost in His Light. I chose to be happy with what I had and what I didn't have because I know that God has every detail of my life under control. I chose to give God my all; my heart, my time, my love, my soul, my body, my mind and I chose to trust Him with it.

I chose to replace my desire for a spouse with an unquenchable desire for God. Single Christian can you make these choices too? If you do, it will change the whole course of your life. God wants you to give Him your all, He wants you to want Him more than anything this earth has to offer you. God wants you to trust Him with your life without questioning Him about everything that He chooses to do with you. Single Christian choosing God means that you choose peace and everlasting love; it means that you choose to trust Him and be happy with whatever He gives you. It means that you will dream big and through God accomplish everything in His will for you.

Choosing God means you choose life and not just any life but life more abundantly. This isn't an altar call, this is God calling you to be at peace with your relationship status, and this is God calling you to trust Him. This is God calling for a deeper relationship with you single Christian and if anyone deserves to know you deeply and intimately its God. He loves you more than anyone in this world and has proven His love from the beginning of time. Choose to marry God first, He deserves you.

About The Author

Tiffany Simone is the owner of Crème De La Pies Inc., a dessert company that she started at the age of 25 years old in Brooklyn, New York where she was born and raised. Tiffany grew up in a Holy Ghost filled Pentecostal church and at the age of 20 years old she answered her call to ministry. Tiffany worked as an I.E.P. Paraprofessional for the New York City Department of Education where she, with her combined love for children, children's books and the Lord, was inspired to write her first book Blake's Bible Adventures: The Story of Moses. After two years as an I.E.P. Paraprofessional, God told her to leave her job to pursue new depths in Him and in ministry, so that is precisely what she did. After leaving her job Tiffany founded a ministry that included a non-denominational open forum bible study, prayer and street ministry. Since then Tiffany moved on to utilize her gifts in greater arena and has become a preacher of the Gospel. She plans on founding several Non- Profit Organizations to help edify people, spread the Word of God and build the Kingdom; she will also be opening a church in the near future. She currently resides in Brooklyn, New York.

This Book Was Published By:

Maximize Publishing Inc.

415-779-6297 or
MaximizePublishingInc@gmail.com

MAXIMIZE PUBLISHING

Retail Price: 15.99